Classroom Drama:
Act it out

Gare Thompson

SCHOLASTIC
Toronto • Sydney • New York • London • Auckland

Scholastic-TAB Publications Ltd,
123 Newkirk Road, Richmond Hill, Ontario, Canada L4C 3G5

Scholastic Inc.
730 Broadway, New York, NY 10003, USA

Ashton Scholastic PTY Limited,
PO Box 579, Gosford, NSW 2250, Australia

Ashton Scholastic Limited
165 Marua Road, Panmure, Aukland 6, New Zealand

Scholastic Publications Ltd.
Holly Walk, Leamington Spa, Warwickshire CV324LS, England

Cover by Jo Huxley

6 5 4 3 2   Printed in USA   9/8 0 1 2 3 4/9

Canadian Cataloguing in Publication Data
Thompson, Gare
    Classroom drama: act it out

ISBN 0-590-71807-X

1. Drama in education. 2. Rhetoric - Study and
teaching (Elementary). 3. Language arts
(Elementary). I. Title.

PS8039.D7T56 1988 372.6'6044   C88-002196-9
PN3171.T56 1988

Contents

Introduction

Drama is one of the oldest forms of communication. Physical action can effectively convey thoughts and feelings (ask anyone who has stood in some foreign village square without command of a word of the native language), and before literacy, people used storytelling and drama to let their contemporaries know what they thought and felt.

Children are natural communicators and dramatists. They come to school with rich imaginations, quicksilver thoughts and feelings, and elastic, active bodies — all natural ingredients for creating plays. Common sense, confirmed by recent research, tells us that reading, writing, talking and listening are *not* separate language arts that need to be taught apart from each other. Drama develops and enriches the same skills as reading and writing: listing, sequencing, character analysis, plot development, drawing conclusions, inferential thinking, recognition of literary concepts, etc.

If you ask a group of children "What happened yesterday?" you'll get a myriad of responses. Some will carefully list *all* the things that happened yesterday, from the time they got up to the time they went to sleep — and if they remember a dream they had, they may even include that! Some will isolate a particularly meaningful event that still occupies their thoughts. Others need coaxing and prompts, by you or by their peers in a trusted group setting. Further direct questions or a modeling of possible responses to the original question, will often elicit the sharing you want.

No matter how hesitant or reluctant some children may seem, they all have a wealth of stories locked inside. And lucky are those who come to you already filled, not only with personal anecdotes, but with the stories of their culture. Those children know about princes and princesses, about the Three Bears, the Five Chinese Brothers, Clifford the dog, and Frances the badger. They ask over and over again to hear and read stories about their favorite characters — often writing stories of their own in response.

But writing isn't the only, or necessarily the best response — stories can also be turned into plays. Through drama, children are sometimes able to explore thoughts and feelings not so easily expressed in telling or writing. From a simple feeling or thought the story can build and layer itself until is has become a tale full of "sound and fury" — something to be enjoyed and shared.

"Fine, I buy the principle," you say. "But does drama really belong in the classroom?"

I say yes. Learning drama techniques will help children become better communicators, honing skills that will be increasingly valuable as they move through school and into other areas of study. Through drama children learn the art of making decisions and segmenting information to use in various ways. More important, they learn that there are many different interpretations of literature, and that their own opinions are valuable and worth sharing. They'll begin to have confidence in their own creative ideas instead of always chasing someone else's "right" answers.

"I'd love to nurture my children's development," you say. "But I've got thirty kids in my class and six different lessons to teach — not to mention preparing the kids for those tests!"

Drama in the classroom doesn't have to be a Broadway production with lights, costumes, thirty-minute scripts, and a cast of thousands. "Reader's theater" needs no elaborate scenery. Children have such vivid imaginations that the skimpiest props can elevate the "mere" telling of a story into a full-fledged play in their eyes.

"All right, I'll give it a try," you say. "But how can I be sure it will it work?"

Trust me, it will work. It's worked for me even at the kindergarten level. One day I was trying to develop a play with a group of young children when it struck me how instinctively they knew what a play was and what we were trying to achieve. We had decided to adapt *The Little Red Hen*. But soon we also had Goldilocks, the Three Bears, Snow White and six of the Seven Dwarfs (no one could remember the name of the seventh) entering and exiting our play to share tea and bread with the Red Hen. Needless to say, the other animals from the original story looked on quite enviously.

How did all those characters suddenly appear in our adaptation? I had simply asked, "If the Little Red Hen was going to throw a party, who do you think she'd invite?" Everyone agreed she wouldn't invite anyone from the story itself because they'd been mean to her and you don't invite mean people to parties. So I asked, "Who would you invite from other stories you know?" They quickly gave me their suggestions, which I listed on the board.

Next I read aloud some "party" scenes from *Alice in Wonderland*, *Where the Wild Things Are*, *Frog and Toad Are Friends* and *What Do You Do With a Kangaroo?* so they could see what characters might say to each other at a party, and what they might do. This naturally led to a discussion about the party we wanted: What kind of party would it be? Who would accept our invitation and who wouldn't? What decorations would we have? What games? We listed all the suggestions next to our list of invitees.

Many of the children volunteered information about parties they'd been to, especially birthday parties. They told us how many children had been there, what had happened, what they liked and disliked. I focused on what they had seen and heard and felt, since those elements would help us develop the dialogue for our party play. Some of the children decided to tape their thoughts and feelings, while others wrote them down.

Now we had established the framework, we needed to begin writing our play. We had defined the party, settled where it would be, established the cast of characters, and decided on the action. Soon dialogue began flowing and the play got underway.

This simple beginning generated a playwriting activity that lasted for two weeks and culminated in a shared performance. Of course a good deal of time was spent editing, rewriting, and finalizing our play before the "curtain" went up, but the children continued to think and invent right into the performance!

A very important by-product was that they developed a new language — the language of drama. Words such as *character*, *setting*, *dialogue*, *monologue*, *plot*, *action*, *director*, *scenery* and *costumes* found their way into daily conversations. The children were building a store of knowledge that would be useful to them throughout their school and adult lives.

Perhaps most important of all, they were experiencing sheer, energetic, motivating, learning-guaranteed fun!

The rest of this guide will set the stage for your very own classroom drama. *All the world's a stage* . . . so on with the show!

Setting the stage: book talk time

Before you can develop plays in your classroom, the children will have to be exposed to many stories — stories they hear read or told, and stories they tell and write themselves. They need to understand stories and how they develop so they can transfer that understanding to their playwriting.

For developing plays with young children I choose books that are already familiar to them, ones I know they enjoy. Stories with straightforward linear plots help them see clearly how plot development affects the characters. Predictable stories like *The Magic Fish* are often especially suitable. The same action (wish/wish fulfillment/ dissatisfaction) is repeated until the disastrous culmination, and the characters react the same way each time. The children have no difficulty seeing the sequence of events.

Many fairy tales have a similar wish-fulfillment sequence. Most folktales are equally predictable, often because events happen in sequences of three. In both, the settings are usually clear and easily accessible for children, and the characters are straightforward. Modern stories often have the advantage of already well-known characters such as Clifford, Frances, and Curious George. Since the children can easily predict what these favorites will say and do, and what is likely to happen to them, they can spend more time and thought on the problem/solution aspects of the story and the shaping of climax and resolution.

I spend a substantial amount of time talking about the books first, to activate the children's prior knowledge. By formulating my questions in a way that will force them to think about their answers, I try to bring out as much useful information as possible, touching on key issues they will need to consider later on. Questions that have simple yes or no answers don't do much to develop the play.

Choosing the book

The following initial approach is fairly standard for most books, and leads to more specific and pointed questions as our discussions develop:

- I point to the cover art and ask, "What do you see happening on the cover?"

- Sometimes I read (or ask one of the children to read) the title, author and illustrator. Then I ask, "What do you think this book will be about?"
- If the main character appears on the cover, I ask, "Who do you think this is?" and "What do you think will happen to this person (animal)?"
- I also like to ask, "Have you read any other stories like this one?"

It's critical to keep track of any predictions. I often use volunteers as "scribes" (they love the word!) to write suggestions down. Some teachers prefer a tape recorder. Very young children can draw pictures of their predictions.

This "note taking" is a process all playwrights go through as they develop a play. It's important for children because it helps them see that drama is simply another form of storytelling. The notes also act as reference points when we're working on character, plot and setting, and help us arrive at the resolution. It's often from them that the title for the play eventually comes.

After we examine the cover, I read the story aloud. I like to read without interruption the first time, and with all the enthusiasm I can muster. I try to change the tone and timbre of my voice for different characters. I don't mind the children joining in on repetitive parts, but I don't stop for questions and observations the first time through. They have to see that the story has a beginning, a middle and an end, and that the characters develop.

Now we spend time with the story. I reread it, this time stopping for whatever questions and comments the children want to voice. I often ask questions myself:

- Who remembers what happens next?
- Why do you think [this character] did [this]?
- Why did [this character] say [this]?
- What does the picture tell you about [this character]?

Again I encourage note taking so we can use the information as we develop the play.

Learning the terms

When the children have an intimate knowledge of a number of likely stories, it's time to begin playwriting. I first introduce the proper terminology to help them understand how a play works and how the elements work together. Within the safe context of solving real problems, even unfamiliar terms quickly become familiar. Moreover, it's important that the children think and feel they are genuine playwrights.

Character

I write the term and its "definition" on the board: *Characters are people (or animals) who appear in the play.*

Next I ask the children to "nominate" characters from their favorite stories (prince, stepmother, witch, Cinderella, etc.). They write their choices on slips of paper, which are collected and placed in a "magic hat" (or plain old paper bag). We pull some names out of the hat and I list them on the board or on chart paper.

Then I ask the children to think of words that describe the characters (mean, kind, helpful, cruel, etc.) and I write them under the character names. If the children have problems thinking up appropriate traits, I share some stories with them. If they've listed "prince," for instance, but can't think of a trait, I read them a fairy tale with a prince in it. Afterwards I ask questions:

- What kind of person was the prince?
- How did he act? Was he brave?
- Would you want him for a friend?

Such prompts help the children think of traits for building their characters.

How many characters do we list? Obviously a play needs at least two. I've found the number doesn't really matter because we can always delete some later, or group them as members of a "chorus." The children soon learn themselves to eliminate characters that aren't necessary to the plot, or that don't fit the other elements of the play. Usually I try to list enough (including a chorus) to involve the whole class. If necessary, several children can share the narrator's part.

Setting

Setting is where the play happens.

I ask the children where they think all the characters might meet, and we brainstorm potential places before settling on one. This discussion may eliminate some of their earlier character suggestions, or perhaps necessitate additional ones. If the children need further help, again I read one of their favorite stories and ask, "Where did this story take place?" They quickly catch on.

Plot

Plot is what happens in the play.

That sounds simple enough, but this is probably the hardest term of all for children to understand. Plot refers to what the characters do, but it must also include a conflict of some kind. If often helps to ask the children, "What is the problem in the play?" or "What problem did [this character] face?"

Once more, if they have problems, I read them a favorite story with a straightforward narrative and a clearly described problem, then ask questions about it. Depending on the age and experience of the group, I may also stress that our play will have three parts:

Act 1: the beginning, the opening
Act 2: the middle, the descripton of the conflict facing the characters
Act 3: the end, the resolution (fairy tales, they will note, always have happy endings!)

Dialogue

Dialogue is what the characters say to each other.

Ask questions like, "What would the prince say to the stepmother?" or "What would Little Red Hen shout to Henny Penny as she goes by?" Most children will readily volunteer bits of dialogue for the characters you listed earlier.

Developing the play

Finally we reinforce the terms learned by putting together the various dramatic elements. Because the atmosphere is safe and enjoyable, by now the children are usually free with their suggestions. I've found the following activities useful:

Freeze play

This activity helps children understand character motivation and the concept of plot.

Ask them to write the name of their favorite character on a piece of paper and put it into the magic hat. Explain that you need two volunteers to draw a name and *improvise* a scene. You may need to explain that when characters improvise they create dialogue as they go, without writing or learning it first.

First ask the class to choose a favorite story about the character picked and think about three things:

- What happens in the story and what part of it do they want to work with?
- What is the chosen character like?
- What setting do they want to use?
- Who will the second character be?

(For instance, a friendly but too curious monkey is rescued in an aquarium by a man in a yellow hat.)

Then the two volunteers act out the scene.

After several pairs of children have volunteered and the class has become fairly comfortable with the routine, tell the children you will *freeze play* the next improvisation — that is, when you say those words the actors will freeze whatever they are doing. While the actors are frozen ask, "What do you think these characters would do next?" Have the volunteers follow any suggestions, then ask, "Did that make sense?" The discussion should make it clear that what the characters do and say in a scene depends on who those characters are and where they are. A prince will act differently at an aquarium than a witch will.

Don't be surprised to find the children playing this game on their own after a while. It's a lot of fun.

What's up, Doc?

In this activity, based on the old "whisper" game, the children create an oral tale. Write the following connective words on the board or chart to help them along: *suddenly, then, next, but, because, happily, over, until, finally.* Then give them the first line(s) of a story and ask them each to add a line. They can add characters or change the plot as they go, so long as the story makes sense. Sometimes I ask one of the children to begin the story instead, either by reading the first sentence from a favorite book or by making one up.

Here are some possible starters:

- Once upon a time there was a beautiful princess who lived in a great big castle. She was lonely because . . .
- In a deep, dark forest there was a tall tree. Suddenly there was a storm . . .
- It was the last inning of the game when Tommy came to bat. The pitcher reared back . . .

Once all those who want to contribute have done so, it's time to review the story. Did it make sense? Was there a beginning, a middle and an end? Were the characters believable? How many settings were there?

Children take to this activity easily and often with great enthusiasm. Sometimes I divide my class into small groups and have each group develop a story and share it with the class.

Critics at large

Various forms of drama, including reader's theater, are becoming popular in schools. A school play, either formal or informal, can provide a great opportunity for children to become reviewers — *after* they are familiar with drama terminology. Or you can present a play (film or video) in the classroom and critique it together.

In the beginning I often model being a reviewer. I try to stress the following:

- Reviewing a play means giving your personal reactions and experiences.
- "Criticism" includes what you liked as well as what you didn't.
- Your opinions have to be validated by reference to the play: Did what happened make sense? Did the dialogue suit the characters?

Critiques can be given orally or in writing — in the children's writing logs, for instance — and shared later, perhaps on a bulletin board, in a classroom published book, or simply in a writing conference. Seeing different reactions to the same work will help children realize that much of drama is subjective, relying on the emotional response it elicits from the audience. It will gradually become clear to them that the more knowledge they have about how a play works, the more they will enjoy and understand it.

Mime

This activity is structured so the children have to create dialogue to complete a play.

We go back and select two characters from our list, decide on a setting, and choose three actions for each of the characters. I steer young children to familiar stories and characters (like Cinderella and the fairy godmother) and help them choose actions by asking, "What happened first? What happened second? What happened last?" (First the fairy godmother changed the pumpkin into a coach, then she changed the mice into horses, etc.)

Explain that the characters are going to act out what happens without using any words, and that action without words is called *mime*. Get two or more volunteers to mime the play.

Then, as the volunteers repeat the presentation, have the children add dialogue. Or have them write the dialogue, individually or in small groups, and later compare their work. Seeing different interpretations of the same action will help the children get used to the notion that their own response to an action can determine a play's outcome.

Summary

These activities function as play activators. They allow the children to experience, explore and challenge the sense of what a play is and what happens in writing one. They become familiar with the language and expectations of playwriting. And they will feel proud that they are creating plays!

Adaptations

I know, let's put on a play! You can be the star, I'll be the director, and everyone will come!
(Mickey Rooney to Judy Garland in *Broadway Babies*.)

The following section includes a number of concrete suggestions based on well-known stories. These are intended as starters and models only, since very soon your children will be choosing and developing their own story-plays. You won't need a huge budget, stars or elaborate props, but you will need a lot of patience, a sense of humor and time to listen to the children.

The Three Billy-Goats Gruff
The book

Some children may already be familiar with this story, but unless all know it well, you should introduce it to the group first. Read the title and show the cover, then ask:

- "Who would appear in a play called *The Three Billy-Goats Gruff?*" Under the heading *Characters*, write their responses, including suggestions for characters *not* found in the original.
- "Where do you think the characters would live?" List the answers under the heading *Setting*.
- "What do you think might happen in the play?" List their responses under the heading *Plot*.

Then brainstorm "billy-goats" to find out what the children know about goats. Write all suggestions down, preferably on an "information about goats" map. (Write *billy-goats* in the center of a circle on the chalkboard, then put the following categories clockwise around it: *friends, enemies, things they learn, places they live*, etc.) The children may want to suggest their own categories as well, and if you leave the map up for a few days, they may add to it as new ideas come to them.

Next read the actual story aloud, with as much enthusiasm as you can muster. (If I can, I avoid the period just after lunch — everyone is too sleepy!) Then discuss together the *characters*, the *plot*, the *setting* and the *dialogue*.

Some children will be ready to plunge into playwriting immediately. Others will need guidance. I usually break the class into groups and ask each group to produce a play, while I circulate as resource person. Within each group *all* children will function as authors. Some will also end up being editors, some stars — and there is usually a budding director, easy to spot!

The play

Some teachers prefer to model the activity first. Here's how I would do it:

"I'm going to make a play based on the book *The Three Billy-Goats Gruff.*" I point to the cover art. "I think I'll have these three billy-goats be the *characters* in my play, and I'll give them these names." Or I ask the children to give them names — one class insisted that Sigfried was a proper name for a goat, but Sebastian was a name for a cat! "The problem in my play is that the goats have to cross a bridge, but a mean troll wants to stop them. I have to figure out a way to get the goats across the bridge. That will be my *plot.*"

While you then sit down to write *your* play, ask the children to write *theirs*. Allow them to adapt freely. Very young children (kindergarten and some first-grade) may produce nothing more than a title and a few lines. Maybe that's all they can think off that day. Honor their work — it's *theirs*. And give them full opportunity to act it out, or perhaps tape it. They'll gain courage and experience from having done it, and they'll continue to learn from their peers.

This free writing may not look much like a play — it doesn't have to. Pirandello's play *Six Characters in Search of an Author* doesn't look like a play either, certainly not the way Arthur Miller's *Death of a Salesman* does. But both tell a story dramatically. *The Telephone* is a forty-five minute monologue with one actress and a telephone — where are the other elements of playwriting there?

We're not trying to teach the formal aspects of playwriting. What is important is that the children recognize drama as another avenue for telling their own stories. For this reason also it's not the time to stress conventions like quotations marks, paragraphing, verb tenses, etc. The more experience the children gather, the more they will play with language to get their meaning clear and the more their writing will begin to approximate the conventional. Verb tenses will become important to them when the order of events becomes important to their play. I can't stress it enough: the play's the thing! And the more fun they have "playing," the more they will learn.

Should you not even think about grammar and punctuation, then? Certainly you should, and there will be "teachable moments" flowing out of your playwriting activities. For example, it's important for the children to know *how* their characters speak:

- The first goat is small and timid. What kind of voice would he use? What kinds of words do timid people use?
- What kind of voice would the troll use to speak to the smallest goat? Would he speak the same way to the biggest goat?
- How many exclamation marks should follow the words *trip-trap*?

The conventions are tools a writer uses to develop meaning as precisely as necessary. Many children invent their own "meaning place-holders" first, and then shift to more conventional usage. To demonstrate the importance of punctuation I sometimes read a story without using any. (*Try* reading *The Three Billy-Goats Gruff* that way — it's almost impossible to do!) The children quickly get the point! At other times I play with sentence strips from stories they know. *Well, come along! I've got two spears, and I'll poke your eyeballs out at your ears* provides possibilities for a good deal of in-context instruction! The important thing is that the children see how their use of particular words, contractions, punctuation, etc. influences the interpretation of their play.

Extensions

Expository writing

After the children write their plays, you may want to have them explore different styles of writing. Dialogue, very important in creating plays, is also much used in the presentation of facts in newscasts. Have the children create and share newscasts of the events on the bridge:

- What happened first? Second? Third?
- Who was involved?
- Who were the victims? (One child insisted the troll was the victim!)
- Where are the goats now? The troll?

Older children could write editorials instead — for instance, on the right of individuals to live where they want (the trolls) and go where they please (the billy-goats).

Points of view

Have the children tell the story from a different point of view:

- What would happen if the troll were the "good guy"?
- What parts of the play would change? Would any part remain the same?
- What dialogue would change?
- What could happen to make the troll the hero of the story? (Could the bridge collapse under the weight of the goats and the troll save them?)
- What would happen if you added another character to the story?

Music and sound effects

Have the children consider what kind of music and sound effects would fit their play:

- What kind of music would best introduce the troll and each of the goats?
- If the characters were musical instruments, what would each be?
- What kind of music would best set the mood at the beginning of the play and signal the end?
- What sounds do the goats make when they cross the bridge?
- What sounds does the troll make?
- What sounds would the play end with?

What if . . . ?

- How would the story change if it took place in the tropics?
- What kind of goats would be in the tropics?
- What would the goats and the troll be wearing if they were in the far north?
- Would a troll live under the bridge if it was very cold?
- What if they lived in outer space?

Older children might also enjoy considering a different time frame: the future, the near or distant past.

Make-believe

Since the goal of the goats is to get fat, ask the children to write menus for a billy-goat restaurant that would help that process along.

(The books *Gregory the Terrible Eater* and *More Spaghetti, I Say!* would be a great sources of ideas, both real and fanciful.)

Observations

When I started working with young children, I thought that most of what I was doing was "over their heads." My own experience in playwriting and theater told me a solid background in language and technique was necessary, and these children clearly hadn't developed that expertise. But they had the last laugh. They quickly understood the rules and requirements of plays and began to develop their own. Playwriting terms became part of their everyday speech. I learned so much from them! Children really do have wonderful stories and plays in them. It's our job as teachers to help them mold those stories into finished products — "finished" as far as you think they can be without turning the children off.

And once they're finished, there's the question of performances. It's best to schedule the performances for specific times. To be fair, I draw names from the magic hat, usually allowing three performances per 45-minute time slot.

Some children love to organize, and you may want to let them arrange a "play marathon," a whole afternoon (or day) of performances. Some can create posters, tickets and programs, others help schedule, others look after props. And of course, some will want to be stars! The rest of the school and the parents can be invited, giving you an opportunity to showcase the variety of play techniques you've worked with: dramatic readings, reader's theater, staged performances, as well as the different genres explored in the plays.

Whatever type of performance is scheduled, I try to keep the scenery and costume demands to an absolute minimum. The imagination of children (and adults!) doesn't need much to fill in the details and get into the world of the play. I keep in mind that most of the fun for children is not in the final performance, but in the activities that lead up to it.

I don't force the children to perform. Some need time to develop enough confidence, and some won't ever take to the lights. Children are different. Some are oral, some are not. Those who aren't will find other ways to express their plays: in someone else's reading or performance, in a "published" class anthology of plays, in a series of storyboards.

The Little Red Hen

For a dramatization of *The Little Red Hen*, costumes aren't necessary. Simple masks of a hen, a goose, a dog and a cat, mounted on sticks and held in front of the actors' faces, might add to the enjoyment, but the essentials of the characters are found in the dialogue. Since the action takes place in a cottage, a few gardening tools and kitchen props might help to stimulate the imagination, and perhaps some seeds and a loaf of bread could be included at the appropriate moments. My rule of thumb is simple: no more props than are necessary to sustain the play.

The storyboard

I use *The Little Red Hen* to model the creation of a storyboard. I first follow the same steps as outlined for *The Three Billy-Goats Gruff*: to explore characters, plot, setting and dialogue, model a playwriting, and ask the children to write their own versions.

Then I ask them to go back and *segment* the plot. Each separate action sequence becomes a storyboard, as shown:

Storyboard 1: Introducing the characters
Introduce the goose (drawing of goose gossiping)
Introduce the cat (drawing of cat preening)
Introduce the dog (drawing of dog sleeping)
Introduce Little Red Hen (drawing of hen working)
Caption: *They all lived in a house in the country.*

Storyboard 2: Planting the seeds . . .

You may want to put the storyboards up around the room as murals. Or, if the size and flexibility of the paper permit, quickly flipping the series of storyboards creates the impression of a film!

The play

Here is a possible adaptation of *The Little Red Hen*.

Characters:
Narrator
Little Red Hen
Goose
Cat

Dog
Neighbors (as many as the director wants)

Setting:
A cottage in the country

Plot:
The Little Red Hen asks for help raising wheat, harvesting it, and then baking bread. Her friends refuse to help until they smell the bread, and then they want to share it. The Little Red Hen decides she deserves all the bread.

Scene I

Narrator:	Once upon a time, in a cottage in the country, there lived a goose, a cat, and a dog. They lived together with the Little Red Hen.
Goose:	*(Talks to neighbors)* I moved in first. And I'm much neater than the dog, who is very messy. Humph! All the cat does is comb her hair or primp. *I* try to help the Little Red Hen. Like now, for instance. I'm staying out of her way while she scrubs the floor. Later I'll tell her if she missed any spots.
Neighbor 1:	How kind of you. You're really a good roommate.
Neighbor 2:	Don't you help her with the chores?
Goose:	Well, I would if I had the time. But you know, I have to tell people what's happening. That takes a lot of my time. And then I have to watch what everyone is doing.
Neighbor 3:	You are a busybody, aren't you?
Goose:	*(Smiles)* Yes, I am!

Scene II

Narrator:	So the goose had no time to help the Little Red Hen. What about the cat and the dog?
Cat:	Oh dear, I just don't know what to wear, although I do look good in everything I put on. Not like that poor Red Hen. She just can't seem to keep her clothes clean. Poor thing!
Dog:	*(Yawns)* I know. And she makes so much noise. That's why I'm always tired. I just can't seem to get a full day's rest. *(Falls asleep)*
Cat:	Well, I think I'll wear my new dress. *(Pulls out dress)* Look at this! *(Wakes up dog)*

Dog:	What?
Cat:	Of all the nerve! The Little Red Hen forgot to iron my dress!
Dog:	Well, at least that will be quiet. Good day! *(Falls asleep again)*
Cat:	I'll have to wear an old dress. I hope Goose doesn't notice. The whole town will know if she does. *(Sighs)* You just can't depend on Red Hen.
Dog:	That's true! *(Snores)*

Scene III

Narrator:	But the poor Little Red Hen just kept working. One day while she was taking the cat's dry-cleaning to town she found some seeds.
Red Hen:	Seeds! Perhaps the others will help me plant them.
Narrator:	She hurried back and showed the others what she had found.
Red Hen:	Look what I've found!
Goose:	What? Did someone lose something? I'll have to find out who it was.
Cat:	Is is something I can wear?
Dog:	Keep quiet! I can never sleep around here!
Red Hen:	It's seeds. We can plant them. Who will help?
Goose:	*(Hurries out the door)* Not I. I'll go and see if any of the neighbors lost them.
Cat:	Not I. I don't have any planting clothes to wear. Besides, I have a hair appointment. Goodbye!
Dog:	Not I. I'm allergic to work — I mean seeds. Sorry.
Red Hen:	Well, I will plant them.

Scene IV

Narrator:	So the Little Red Hen planted her seeds. She watered them and took care of them until it was time to harvest them.
Red Hen:	Who will help me harvest the wheat?
Goose:	Not I. But I will tell the neighbors that the wheat is ready.
Cat:	Not I. I don't have a straw hat and the sun is much too hot. I'm going to take a cool bath.
Dog:	Not I. I really have to finish last night's dream.

Scene V

Narrator:	And so the Little Red Hen harvested the wheat all by herself. Then she took it to the miller. Finally she brought the flour home.
Red Hen:	I planted the seeds. I harvested the wheat. I took the grain to the miller. I brought the flour back. Now who will help me bake the bread?
Goose:	Not I. But I will tell everyone you are going to bake delicious bread.
Cat:	Not I. I don't have an apron to match my eyes.
Dog:	Not I. I have my best dreams on cool days like this.
Red Hen:	Then I'll bake the bread by myself.

Scene VI

Narrator:	And the Little Red Hen baked the bread all by herself.
Red Hen:	*(Smiles)* The bread is baked. Now who will help me eat it?
Goose:	Oh, I will. And I won't tell anyone!
Cat:	Oh, I will. I'm already dressed for a party!
Dog:	Oh, I will. And I'll dream about it afterwards.
Red Hen:	You will? Who planted the wheat and harvested it? I did. Who took the wheat to the miller and brought it back again? I did. Who baked the bread? I did. And now I'm going to eat the bread all by myself!
Narrator:	And so she did. The goose went outside and told everyone. The cat changed into mourning clothes. And the dog had a nightmare. But the Little Red Hen was very happy.

You may use this adaptation of ours in any way you wish, but you'll have more fun if you write one of your own. And the children will have more fun if *they* write *their* own.

Extensions

Hen party

Have the children draw up a guest list for Red Hen's party, make the invitations, plan the menu, decide on the gifts, and arrange the seating. Allow each child to choose a "friend" to invite as well. (I usually specify stuffed animals since one time I had a live zoo in class for the day!) Have them improvise dialogue among the invitees.

Friendship Day

First have the children develop a list of the qualities that make a good friend. Then say to them, "If you could choose one thing to share with a friend, what would it be?" Drawings, favorite toys, stories — whatever they bring, put everything into a large "friendship box." On Friendship Day open the box and share what's inside, along with some favorite (or new) friendship stories.

Around the world

Have each child pick a different country or region and research what kind of bread would come from there: sourdough from Ireland (or San Francisco), bagels from New York, pita from Morroco, chow fan from China, matzoh from Israel. Have them create plays set in their chosen countries, or make a large map with drawings of the different breads in the appropriate locations.

Change characters

What other characters could be added to the play, and how would they affect it? For instance, Frog and Toad would probably help the Little Red Hen, but what would happen if Curious George were added? What might Red Hen say in an advertisement for new roommates? Who might answer the ad?

Cinderella
The scene

Like folktales, fairy tales are readily adaptable into plays. But the language of fairy tales is unique — "once upon a time" opens the curtain to a world filled with magic, evil, enchantment and danger. But we are safe to work with it: the ending is always happy!

It is fun (though sometimes tricky!) to have children develop the reality of fairy tale characters using their own experiences. For example, Cinderella has a stepmother and stepsisters who don't treat her very well, and there is no mention of her father. A fairy godmother intervenes to make sure there is justice in Cinderella's life. A substantial number of children in today's society have to learn how to cope with step-families, so don't be surprised if that reality seeps into your script. Only you can judge how explicit the question can be made for your children. In Cinderella's family there is jealousy and power struggle which all readers, from step-families or not, are likely to have experienced. A play can illustrate and heighten the child's cry for justice.

Current events can also contribute to a "modern" version — for instance, the media-romanticized fairy tale of Diana, the Princess of Wales. Why could (or couldn't) Diana be considered a modern Cinderella? What would a modern Cinderella be like? What inventions would make her life easier? How would her sisters show their jealousy? Would her wedding be televised? Could those elements be incorporated into a modern Cinderella play?

Because fairy tales are quite long, it's usually better to adapt particular scenes separately rather than attempt the whole tale. This will allow the children to be more critical of character development and plot nuances. Or you might have different groups work on separate scenes and later join them into a class play.

The wedding scene in *Cinderella* is rich with possibilities:

Characters: Who would be the guests? Who would sit together and who would be kept apart?
Dialogue: What would the characters say to each other?
Plot: How would Cinderella's stepmother and stepsisters act?
Setting: Where would the wedding take place?

To flesh out the details and enrich the key dramatic elements of the play, the children might also consider the following:

- What kind of music would be played?
- What would the guests wear?
- What kinds of gifts would the various guests bring?
- What would the invitations say?
- What flower arrangments and toasts would be appropriate?

The play

Characters:
Cinderella
Prince
Stepmother
Stepsister I
Stepsister II

Father
Fairy Godmother
King
Queen
Snow White and husband
Sleeping Beauty and husband
Assorted guests

Setting:
Cinderella's favorite restaurant, deep in the forest but not too far from the palace. Lots of seafood.

Plot:
Everyone has a good time and makes friends, even the two stepsisters.

Narrator:	Guests, gather round your tables. Please find your seats. There are name cards.
Snow White:	I hope they don't serve apple pie for desert!
Her husband:	Don't worry, I'll eat yours.
Queen:	You don't suppose Sleeping Beauty will fall asleep during the meal, do you?
King:	I hope not.
Narrator:	Welcome Cinderella's sisters — I mean her stepsisters.
Stepsister I:	I want to sit next to Cinderella.
Stepsister II:	I want to.
I:	No, I do.
II:	We both will.
Stepmother:	Yes, do sit next to your dear sister. After all, she's marrying you off to the prince's brothers.
Narrator:	Please rise for Cinderella and the prince. *(Everyone applauds)*
Cinderella:	Thank you all for coming. I love the fine gifts you gave me.
Prince:	Yes, you've made us very happy. We now have slippers for every day of the year.
Stepmother:	I would like to propose a toast: May you live happily ever after!
Sleeping Beauty:	I've heard that one before!

I must admit, I wrote this for my own amusement. The thing is, once children realize that adaptations are *their* stories, they'll play with the possibilities, suppose their own Cinderalla party, introduce their own favorite characters, set up their own plot. Perhaps they will:

- have Cinderella open her gifts
- have the prince try all the slippers on his bride's feet
- have the characters each propose a toast
- have the stepsisters meet their future husbands
- have Snow White and Sleeping Beauty trade dreams

Non-fiction

There is no reason to limit adaptations to pieces of fiction. Books like *The New Baby Calf* and *Have You Seen Birds?*, while written in playful and lyrical language, are pieces of expository writing. Such books easily become the basis of documentaries and news stories. "Scenes" would have to be set with greater attention to factual detail; the "plot" would describe an event rather than a conflict; the "dialogue" would be reporting, not conversation.

For example, *The New Baby Calf* informs the reader about the stages a calf goes through while learning to be independent. The book gives the facts, in text and illustrations:

- The baby calf learns to walk.
- It is hard to learn to walk, and it takes a while.
- The calf needs milk and other food to grow strong.
- There are other animals on the farm.
- The farmer keeps a sharp eye on the calf and its mother.

The children can use these facts to create a news report or dramatization: *A day in the life of a new baby calf.* Not only would the children be entertained, the factual information would be enhanced and enriched. A natural extension activity would be to share newspaper or magazine articles or watch a TV news program to become better acquainted with reporting styles.

Contemporary fiction

Using favorite characters as the basis for plays allows the children to place characters familiar to them in different situations and predict their actions and dialogue.

Curious George, Frog and Toad, Amelia Bedelia and Clifford are well-defined characters, and children have no trouble predicting what they will do in various situations. Everyone knows that Curious George is curious, gets into trouble, and is always rescued by the man in the yellow hat. Amelia's literal interpretation of language is what gets her into trouble, and Clifford has problems with his size. Frog and Toad remain friends no matter how much they argue and misunderstand each other.

By asking the children to invent new stories for these characters, you give them opportunities to develop a real sense of story, of plot and setting. One way is to create two lists, one of settings and one of favorite characters. Then ask the children, individually or in small groups, to pick one item from each list (or draw one of each from the magic hat) and create a short play using the selected setting and character. Give them time to brainstorm possibilities first, then ask for improvisations, or a mime with the subsequent addition of written dialogue.

Conclusion

Classroom drama allows children to think out loud and practice the elements of storytelling. Its primary goal is to provide children with opportunities to express their feelings and thoughts in a form that suits the classroom.

There are also a large number of secondary (and important!) benefits:

- Drama serves as a tool to foster reading and writing competencies.
- Drama opens the door for children to experience literature in a variety of ways.
- Drama allows children to share what they know with others.
- Drama enables children to become better acquainted with the language and structures of stories and plays: characters, setting, plot, dialogue, costumes, props.
- Drama develops a number of important specific language skills, especially story technique, vocabulary enrichment and elements of punctuation.
- Drama makes school fun! (Please don't tell the principal.)

So, BREAK A LEG!

Titles in the New Directions series

Each book in the New Directions series deals with a single, practical classroom topic or concern, teaching strategy or approach. Many teachers have recognized the collegial and encouraging tone in them — not surprising, since most of them have been written by practicing teachers. Indeed, if you have an idea for a New Directions title of your own, we encourage you to contact the Publishing Division, Scholastic Canada.

Existing titles include:

In Canada, order from: Scholastic-TAB Publications Ltd., 123 Newkirk Road, Richmond Hill, ON L4C 3G5

In the United States, order from: Scholastic Inc., Box 7502, Jefferson City, MO 65102